beautiful
wreaths
& garlands

beautiful
wreaths
& garlands

35 projects to decorate
your home for all seasons & occasions

catherine woram

CICO BOOKS
LONDON NEW YORK

LONDON BOROUGH OF WANDSWORTH	
9030 00004 0748 8	
Askews & Holts	06-Nov-2014
745.926	£12.99
	WWX0012901/0064

Published in 2014 by CICO Books
an imprint of Ryland Peters & Small
341 E 116th St, New York, NY 10029
20–21 Jockey's Fields, London WC1R 4BW

www.rylandpeters.com

10 9 8 7 6 5 4 3 2 1
Text © Catherine Woram 2014
Design and photography © CICO Books 2014

ISBN: 978 1 78249 152 1

Printed in China

Copy Editor: Caroline West
Designer: Laura Woussen
Photography: Penny Wincer
In-house Editor: Anna Galkina
Art director: Sally Powell
Production Controller: Sarah Kulasek-Boyd
Publishing manager: Penny Craig
Publisher: Cindy Richards

contents

introduction

Wreaths and garlands are a lovely way to adorn your home and outdoor living space, providing the perfect decoration for special occasions like Valentine's Day, Easter, Hallowe'en, Thanksgiving, and, of course, Christmas. However, wreaths and garlands are not merely for festive celebrations—they are versatile objects that transcend the seasons and make wonderful decorative features at birthday parties, weddings, and summer garden parties.

In this book you will find a wealth of ideas for creating wreaths and garlands of every kind, including a Beachcomber's Garland, hung with seashells and starfish, and a Succulent Candle Wreath studded with fresh succulents. There are also inspirational ideas for designing wreaths and garlands for every room in the home, whether this is a Bay Leaf Wreath decorated with dried chili peppers for hanging in the kitchen, which is perfect for the dedicated cook, or a Scented Eucalyptus Wreath with fragrant leaves to display in a bathroom.

So many different materials can be used to make wreaths and garlands, from the more obvious fresh flowers (such as peonies, hydrangeas, and lavender) and evergreen foliage, including myrtle, holly, ivy, and sweet bay which you may have in your garden, to more unusual materials like driftwood twigs, cotton fabrics, and decorative floral papers and newsprint.

I do hope you will find inspiration in this book and that you enjoy making the wreaths and garlands as much as I did, whether to decorate your own home or to give as gifts to friends and family.

techniques

Wiring plant stems, leaves, and sprigs of foliage to a wreath frame

To wire a plant stem: You will need fine florist's wire, which you can buy in 4in (10cm) lengths. Before wrapping the wire around the stem, you can also insert a piece of wire through the stem to strengthen it. Fold a length of wire in half, wrap it once or twice around the stem, and then wrap the wire around the wreath frame. Twist the ends of the wire together tightly to attach the stem to the wire and trim the ends with scissors or wire cutters.

To wire a leaf: Wrap a length of wire around the leaf stalk (as for wiring a stem above), but do not insert a piece of wire through the stalk.

To wire a sprig of foliage or berries: These are attached to a wreath frame in the same way as plant stems and leaves, but you will need to use slightly thicker wire which is stronger and more capable of holding the weight of the foliage and berries. Wrap the wire around the base of the sprig of foliage or berries (as for wiring a stem above) and attach to the frame by twisting the ends of the wire together. You may also wish to use some finer wire to attach the top of the foliage or berries to the wreath to stop them bending or flopping down.

Cutting wire

The tool you use for cutting wire will depend on the thickness of wire you are using. Fine florist's wire can be cut with scissors, but you will need wire cutters for wires that are any thicker. Always be careful when cutting wire because the ends can be quite sharp.

Stitching a length of ribbon to create a hanging loop

Cut the ribbon to the required length for your wreath. Fold the ribbon in half, pass it underneath the wreath, and thread the ends of the ribbon through the loop. Pull tightly so that the ribbon fits snugly around the wreath. Bring the ends of the ribbon together and trim them so that they are exactly the same length. Fold the ends of the ribbon to the inside and stitch together using whip stitch (see Useful Stitches, page 8).

Hanging wreaths and garlands

Using cup hooks: The easiest way to hang a wreath or garland is to fix a cup hook to the wall or area where you wish to hang the decoration (you will need one hook for a wreath and two hooks for a garland). If the surface is made from wood (e.g. a door or panel), you will be able to screw the cup hook directly into the material. If it is made from plaster or brick (e.g. a wall), then you will need to use rawl plugs, an electric drill, and appropriately sized screws. The heavier the wreath or garland, the larger the cup hooks will need to be.

Using S hooks: S hooks are often known as butcher's hooks and are a simple way of creating a hook for suspending a wreath from string or ribbon above a table (see, for example, the Hanging Ivy Wreath on page 114). Once you have attached the lengths of string or ribbon for hanging to the sides of the wreath, pull the ends together so that they are of equal length. Fold all the ends over by around ¾in (2cm) and stitch them together. This will create a loop

in the ribbons for inserting the S hook. Then attach the top of the S hook to a ceiling hook or the branch of a light or chandelier (see below).

Suspending a decoration above a table: Should you wish to hang a wreath or garland above a table, you can fix a hook or hooks to the ceiling and suspend the decoration from there. Alternatively, try attaching it to an existing light fitting (e.g. the branch of a chandelier) for a more temporary fixing. Make sure the light fitting is strong enough to support the weight of the wreath or garland.

Drilling holes in seashells

Seashells are quite delicate, but with care you can drill holes in them. Mark the position of the hole with a pencil and place a small piece of masking tape over the pencil mark. This will stop the drill bit slipping on the shiny surface of the shell as you drill. Use a very fine drill bit and an electric drill on a slow setting and carefully drill the hole in the required place. Remove the masking tape and thread the string, ribbon, or wire through the hole in the shell.

useful stitches

Some of the projects use specific stitches to create the best results. The following instructions provide step-by-step guidance for making these stitches.

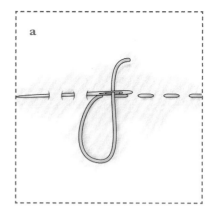

Running stitch

This is the basic stitch used in hand-sewing and consists of a line of small, even stitches that do not overlap.

Fig a

1 Secure the end of the thread at the back of the fabric with a few small stitches.

2 Push the needle down through the fabric a little way along and then bring it back up through the fabric a stitch length along. Repeat to form a row of stitches.

Whip stitch

A traditional stitch for sewing together two layers of fabric or stitching closed an opening in fabric.

1 Tie a knot in the end of the thread and push the needle up through the top layer of fabric—this will conceal the knot on the inside of the fabric.

2 Push the needle through both layers of fabric in almost the same position as the knot—this will ensure the stitching does not loosen where the knot is positioned.

Fig b

3 Push the needle through the two layers of fabric, about ¼in (5mm) away from the first stitch. Continue to work this stitch and the stitches will become slightly angled and cover the layers of the fabric opening.

4 When you have finished sewing, fasten off by making several stitches together. Trim the ends of the thread carefully using scissors.

Blanket stitch

This stitch is used to reinforce the edge of thicker fabrics (it was traditionally used to edge blankets).

1 Bring the needle through at the edge of the fabric.

2 Push the needle back through the fabric a short distance from the edge and loop the thread under the needle. Pull the needle and thread as far as you can to make the first stitch. **Fig c**

3 Make another stitch to the right of this and again loop the thread under the needle. Continue along the fabric and finish with a few small stitches or a knot on the underside. **Fig d**

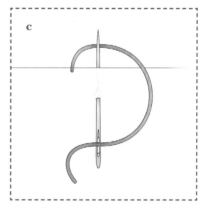

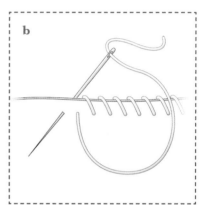

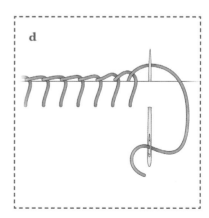

tools and materials

The following is a list of suggestions for the various tools and other pieces of equipment that you may find useful when creating wreaths and garlands.

Butcher's twine

Hand pruners (secateurs)

Hooks (for hanging)

Hot glue gun (or all-purpose glue)

Latex (rubber) gloves (for handling prickly/irritant plant material)

Needle and thread

Paintbrush

Paper, pencil, and pieces of card (for making templates)

Pliers

Rope

Ruler

Scissors

Selection of ribbons in different fabrics, colors, and widths (for hanging wreaths and creating garlands)

S hook (for hanging wreaths)

Sharp knife

Spools of different wires:

Copper wire

Fine wire

Florist's wire

Paper-covered florist's wire

Thin wire

String

White (PVA) glue

Wire cutters

Different types of wreath

Wreaths are available in a range of shapes and sizes, but usually fall into one of two categories: single-framed wreaths (hoops) and wire wreath frames (which have two or more frames). You can, of course, buy ready-woven wreaths, as well as wreaths made from different materials:

Wreath Hoops (in a range of diameters):

Wire wreath hoop

Paper-covered wreath hoop

Polystyrene hoop

Wire Wreath Frames (in a range of diameters):

Circular wire wreath frame

Square wire wreath frame

Heart-shaped wire wreath frame

Ready-woven wreaths

Useful plant materials

Foliage plants such as Norway spruce, blue spruce, pine, juniper, cedar, silver fir, holly, ivy, sweet bay leaves, eucalyptus, rosemary, myrtle, magnolia leaves, photinia leaves, as well as twigs that bend (for creating wreaths from scratch)

Decorating wreaths

Mother-of-pearl buttons, colored buttons, berry picks, frosted pine picks, wired pine cones, ivy leaves (real and artificial), sprigs of herbs (such as lavender and rosemary), dried chili peppers, feathers, sequins, fabric flowers, paper flowers, seashells, starfish, candle clips and candles, small bells.

chapter one

leaves & flowers

rosemary
heart wreath

This fragrant wreath, with its simple, heart-shaped design, would look lovely in any room. Decorated with tiny, flower-shaped leaf clusters and hung from a simple ribbon, three of these wreaths would look great displayed together in a row, perhaps in a window.

materials

Branches of fresh rosemary

Scissors or hand pruners (secateurs)

Heart-shaped wire wreath frame

Fine wire

Pliers

Flower-shaped leaf clusters or other small leaves, such as variegated boxwood (*Buxus sempervirens* 'Variegata'), *Euonymous*, and *Elaeagnus* 'Quicksilver')

10in (25cm) oatmeal-colored ribbon, ½in (1cm) wide, for hanging

1 Cut the rosemary branches into lengths of approximately 25cm (10cm), using scissors or hand pruners, and put them to one side.

2 Start by laying the lengths of rosemary around the wire frame and use pieces of fine wire to bind them securely to the frame. Twist the ends of the wire together to ensure the rosemary is firmly attached. Trim the ends of the wire with the pliers.

3 Continue to attach the lengths of rosemary to the wire frame until it is completely covered, remembering to trim the ends of the wire with the pliers. Tie short lengths of wire to the smaller leaves and attach these to the wreath in the same way.

4 Tie the ribbon to the top of the wreath and knot securely to form a hanging loop. Trim the ends of the ribbon diagonally with the scissors to stop them fraying.

succulent candle wreath

This architectural wreath makes a striking center-piece for a table. The waxy-leaved succulents will also remain lush and vibrant, even on a hot summer's day.

materials

Piece of poultry netting (chicken wire), approximately 8 x 12in (20 x 30cm)

Wire cutters

Damp moss

Latex (rubber) gloves

Florist's wire

German pins (for pinning the pieces of moss)

Selection of succulent plants, including *Crassula ovata* (money plant), *Echeveria,* and *Schlumbergera* (Christmas cactus)

Pillar candles

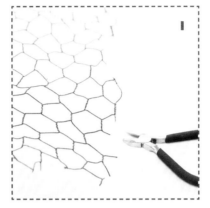

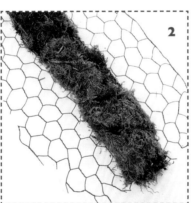

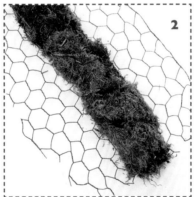

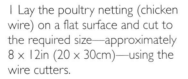

1 Lay the poultry netting (chicken wire) on a flat surface and cut to the required size—approximately 8 x 12in (20 x 30cm)—using the wire cutters.

2 Lay the moss on top of the netting and squeeze it into a sausage shape. Continue to add more pieces of moss along the netting and squeeze them into shape. (You may prefer to wear a pair of gloves to do this because it can be a messy job.)

3 Wrap the netting around the moss sausage shape and pull it tightly to form a tube. Use small lengths of florist's wire to hold the netting in place and twist the ends of the wire several times to secure them.

4 Bend the moss sausage into a circular shape and then use more wire to join the ends together. Twist the wire around the shape to ensure it is fixed securely. Trim the ends of the wire with the wire cutters.

5 Carefully remove the leaves and rosettes from the succulent plants, and use German pins to fix them to the moss ring.

6 Gently lift the leaves of the succulent rosettes and insert the pins beneath the leaves so that they do not show.

7 Attach the leaves all around the moss ring, using German pins to hold them in place, and continue to add more leaves to ensure the whole ring is covered.

8 Continue to cover the top, outside, and inside of the wreath with leaves and rosettes, fixing them in place with German pins. Lay the finished wreath on a table and fill with pillar candles to finish.

(Safety note: never leave lit candles unattended.)

Instead of succulents, try using a selection of roses—perhaps in soft pastel shades or with a lovely fragrance—to create a more ephemeral and summery display

heart
chair-back wreath

This delicate, heart-shaped, twig wreath is sprayed white and decorated with fragrant dried rosebuds. You can use these wreaths to decorate the backs of chairs—they look particularly lovely at a wedding or garden party.

materials

Selection of fine and thicker twigs

Heart-shaped wire wreath frame, approximately 8in (20cm) across at the widest point

Florist's wire

White spray paint

Dried rosebuds

Hot glue gun (or all-purpose glue)

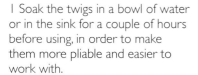

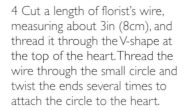

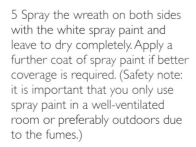

1 Soak the twigs in a bowl of water or in the sink for a couple of hours before using, in order to make them more pliable and easier to work with.

2 Take a small bunch of the twigs and bend them around one half of the wire wreath frame. Use lengths of florist's wire to fix the twigs to the frame, wrapping the wires around several times and twisting the ends to keep them in place.

3 Repeat on the opposite side of the wire wreath frame using more lengths of florist's wire. Then take one of the twigs and bend it carefully to form a circle with a diameter of about 2in (5cm). Weave the ends of the twig into t he circle to keep them in position.

4 Cut a length of florist's wire, measuring about 3in (8cm), and thread it through the V-shape at the top of the heart. Thread the wire through the small circle and twist the ends several times to attach the circle to the heart.

5 Spray the wreath on both sides with the white spray paint and leave to dry completely. Apply a further coat of spray paint if better coverage is required. (Safety note: it is important that you only use spray paint in a well-ventilated room or preferably outdoors due to the fumes.)

6 Take the dried rosebuds and choose the best ones to create the flower design. Use glue or a hot glue gun to fix the first rosebud in place and start creating the flower. You will need to stick five rosebuds to the heart-shaped frame to create the flower. Stick a further rosebud to the center of the flower to finish.

scented eucalyptus wreath

Make this simple yet effective wreath using eucalyptus branches and sprigs of lavender—the steam in a bathroom will release the essential oils in the eucalyptus leaves to emit a lovely fragrance.

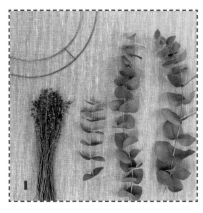

materials

Scissors

Branches of fresh eucalyptus

Pliers

Florist's wire

Circular wire wreath, with a double rim, 12in (30cm) in diameter

Stems of fresh lavender

1 Use the scissors to cut the eucalyptus branches into shorter lengths so that you have about 30 to 40 stems. Use the pliers to cut lengths of florist's wire, each measuring approximately 8in (20cm), and set these to one side.

2 Place a stem of eucalyptus on the outside rim of the wire wreath and wrap a piece of florist's wire around the end to secure it in place. Gently bend the eucalyptus stem to follow the curve of the wire and use more lengths of florist's wire to attach it to the wreath. Repeat until the outside rim of the wreath is covered with eucalyptus.

3 Repeat the process on the inside rim of the wreath, using lengths of florist's wire to attach the eucalyptus stems and making sure you twist the ends of the wire together several times to keep them in place.

4 Cut four to five stems of lavender and trim the ends so that they are about 2in (5cm) long. Tie a length of florist's wire around the ends of the lavender stems and attach them to the wreath with more florist's wire. Make sure you twist the ends of the wire several times so that the stems are securely fixed to the wreath. Attach more bunches of lavender around the wreath to finish. Display the wreath by hanging it from a sturdy nail or hook in the wall.

Hang this wreath in a steam-filled bathroom and relieve mental fatigue with the scent of eucalyptus essential oil

Miniature myrtle wreaths

You can use delicate plants such as myrtle and rosemary to create these miniature decorative wreaths finished with pretty ribbons. Using plants with scented foliage will give the wreaths even more impact.

materials

Hand pruners (secateurs)

Sprigs of leaves (such as myrtle, thyme, pine, lavender, and rosemary)

Fine wire

Small wreath hoop, approximately 4in (10cm) in diameter

Pliers

12in (30cm) oatmeal-colored ribbon, approximately ¼in (5mm) wide

Scissors

Hot glue gun (or all-purpose glue)

1 Use the hand pruners (secateurs) to cut off short sprigs, each measuring approximately 4–5in (10–13cm) in length, from your chosen plant.

2 Wrap fine wire around the plant stem and hoop, bending the stem gently to follow the curve of the hoop. Gently fan out the leaves of the plant as you go so that the wire does not flatten them.

3 Continue bending the stem around the hoop, securing it in place with the fine wire. Wrap the wire around the top of the hoop several times in order to secure the final section. Trim the ends of the wire with the pliers.

4 Cut a piece of ribbon, approximately 8in (20cm) in length, and fold it in half. Thread the ribbon through the wreath hoop and pull the ends of the ribbon to secure.

5 Tie a knot at the end of the ribbon to form a hanging loop and cut the ends diagonally with the scissors to stop them fraying. Make a small bow from the remaining length of ribbon and stick this to the front of the hoop using glue or a hot glue gun.

In Greek mythology, Aphrodite is often depicted wearing a myrtle wreath

fresh
flower garland

Floral foam is so simple to use and is perfect for making this professional-looking table garland, which combines pretty flowers like hydrangeas and peonies with fragrant roses and freesias, as well as herbs such as eucalyptus and rosemary.

materials

Scissors

Rectangular block of floral foam, approximately 5 x 10in (13 x 25cm)

Selection of fresh flowers, such as hydrangeas, freesias, antirrhinum, roses, tamarisk, and peonies

Stems of fresh eucalyptus and rosemary

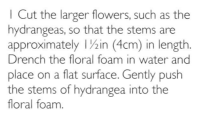

1 Cut the larger flowers, such as the hydrangeas, so that the stems are approximately 1½in (4cm) in length. Drench the floral foam in water and place on a flat surface. Gently push the stems of hydrangea into the floral foam.

2 Cut more flower stems and gently push them into the top of the floral foam. Make sure you cover the foam with flowers so that it does not show in the finished display.

3 Continue to fill the floral form with flowers and then cut more stems to fill the sides, making sure all four sides of the foam are completely covered.

4 Cut the eucalyptus stems and rosemary into lengths of around 8–12in (20–30cm). Push them into the two shorter sides of the floral foam to give the table garland its elongated shape. Place the finished garland in the center of a table on a similar-sized platter and remember to water it regularly to keep the flowers from wilting.

twiggy hydrangea wreath

This delightfully rustic wreath makes a great addition to an outdoor gate, perhaps for a garden party, or hang from a door or on a wall as a spring decoration.

materials

Selection of twigs, approximately 32in (80cm) in length

String

Scissors

3 fresh hydrangea flowers (with stalks attached)

Florist's wire

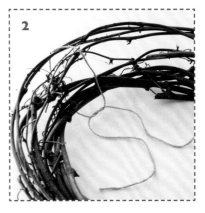

1 Bend the twigs to form a circular wreath shape, approximately 14in (35cm) in diameter. Tie the twigs securely with a length of string to keep them in position. Trim the ends of the string with the scissors.

2 Continue to bend the twigs to form the finished wreath shape and tie the twigs in place with more lengths of string.

3 Take the first hydrangea flower and cut down the stalk so that it is approximately 2in (5cm) in length. Cut a length of florist's wire, measuring about 8in (20cm), and fold it in half. Twist the wire around the hydrangea stalk and then thread it through the twigs. Twist the wire several times to attach the flower securely to the wreath.

4 Cut another length of wire, approximately 8in (20cm) in length, and twist this around the second hydrangea stalk. As before, twist the wire around the twigs to attach the flower to the wreath. Repeat for the third hydrangea. Cut a length of string, about 12in (30cm) in length, and thread it through one of the twigs at the top of the wreath. Tie the ends of the string in a knot to form the hanging loop.

bay leaf wreath

This decorative wreath would make a striking yet practical feature in the kitchen, with its array of bay leaves and colorful dried chili peppers. Keep the wreath close by the stove so that it's always to hand for cooking —the fragrant bay leaves will smell great, too.

materials

Wire wreath hoop, 12in (30cm) in diameter

Stems of fresh *Laurus nobilis* (sweet bay)

Florist's wire

Wire cutters or a strong pair of scissors

Dried chili peppers

Stems of dried herbs, such as rosemary, sage, and thyme (optional)

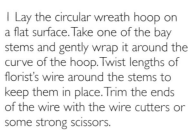

1 Lay the circular wreath hoop on a flat surface. Take one of the bay stems and gently wrap it around the curve of the hoop. Twist lengths of florist's wire around the stems to keep them in place. Trim the ends of the wire with the wire cutters or some strong scissors.

2 Continue to wrap the stems of bay leaf around the wreath hoop, using lengths of florist's wire to hold them in position. Continue in this way until the wreath is full and the wire hoop is completely covered. Trim the loose ends of wire with the wire cutters or scissors.

3 Take a length of wire and wrap it around the stems of the chili peppers. You will need to tie about three chili peppers together and twist the wire several times to keep them secure. Remember to leave enough wire for attaching the chili peppers to the wire wreath hoop.

4 Position the bunch of chili peppers at the top of the wreath and twist the ends of the wire around the wreath hoop to keep it in place. You could also add bunches of dried herbs to fill the wreath if required.

Flower and herb wreath

This lovely and fragrant wreath is made from rustic, dark brown twigs and decorated with a selection of colorful summer flowers that are interspersed with sprigs of rosemary and mint.

materials

Dark wood twigs (for making the wreath framework)

Florist's wire

Large flowers such as peonies and hydrangeas

Scissors

Artificial ready-wired pink berry picks

Pliers (optional)

Stems of fresh rosemary and mint

Small delicate flowers such as *Alchemilla mollis* (lady's mantle) for the wreath surround

20in (50cm) ribbon, ¾in (2cm) wide, for the hanging loop

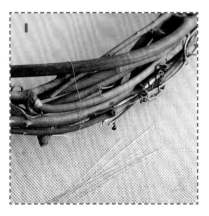

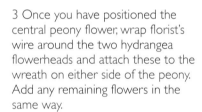

3 Once you have positioned the central peony flower, wrap florist's wire around the two hydrangea flowerheads and attach these to the wreath on either side of the peony. Add any remaining flowers in the same way.

4 Wrap the wire on the berry picks around the wreath and twist the ends several times to keep them in place. Trim the ends of the wire with pliers or scissors.

5 Cut the stems of rosemary and mint into lengths measuring about 4–6in (10–15cm) and wire the ends with florist's wire. Twist the wire around the twigs of the wreath to hold the stems firmly in place.

6 Cut the stems of *Alchemilla mollis* (lady's mantle) into short lengths of about 2–4in (5–10cm) and tuck these into the twigs to hold them in position. You can also use florist's wire to hold them in place if required.

1 Bend the twigs to form a circular wreath shape with a diameter of approximately 14in (35cm) or whatever size is required. You will find it easier to bend the twigs if you soak them in water for a few hours first, as this will make them softer and more pliable. Use lengths of florist's wire to hold the twigs in place to form the wreath.

2 Cut down the large flower stems to a length of about 4in (10cm) using the scissors. Wrap a length of florist's wire around the peony stem and then attach this to the twig wreath, wrapping the wire around several times to keep the flower in place.

7 Fold the ribbon in half, place around the top of the wreath, and pull both ends through the loop. Pull the ribbon tightly around the wreath and knot the ends of the ribbon to form the hanging loop. Trim the ribbon ends diagonally using the scissors to prevent the ends from fraying.

chapter two

fabric & ribbon

fabric heart garland

This pretty heart garland is made using vintage-style fabrics with delicate floral designs. You can create a longer garland by adding more fabric hearts to decorate the top of a doorway or a fireplace.

materials

Paper and pencil
(for the heart templates)

Scissors

Printed cotton fabrics,
approximately 12 x 10in
(30 x 25cm), for each heart

Pins

Sewing machine

Polyester fiber stuffing (for
the hearts)

Needle and thread
40in (1m) ribbon, ½in
(1cm) wide

8 mother-of-pearl buttons

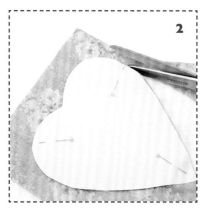

1 Using the templates on page 123, trace the three heart motifs onto a piece of paper with the pencil and cut them out with the scissors. Fold the pieces of fabric in half. Pin the largest heart template to one of the fabric pieces and cut out.

2 Use the three paper templates to cut out two large hearts, one medium heart, and four smaller hearts, each with two layers of fabric.

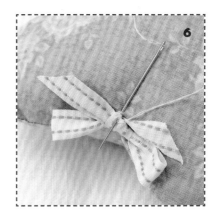

3 With right sides facing, use the sewing machine to stitch the heart shapes together around the edge, leaving a seam of approximately ½in (1cm). Leave an opening of about 1¼in (3cm) along the straight edge of one side of each heart. Trim and notch the edges of the fabric with the scissors.

4 Turn the heart right side out and press flat. Insert the stuffing into the opening—you may find it easier to use the end of a pencil or knitting needle to do this. Push the stuffing carefully into the pointed bottom and the top curves of the heart so that it is evenly distributed.

5 Fold the raw edges of the fabric of the opening toward the inside and use the needle and thread to sew the opening closed with tiny whip stitches. Carefully fasten off your hand-sewing. Repeat for the remaining heart shapes.

6 For each heart, make a small bow from the ribbon and cut the ribbon ends diagonally with scissors to stop the edges fraying. Sew a bow to the top center of each heart with the needle and thread.

7 Neatly stitch the hearts together at the sides with the needle and thread to create the garland shape. Sew a mother-of-pearl button between each heart to cover over the stitching.

8 Cut two pieces of ribbon, approximately 20in (50cm) in length, fold each in half, and hand-stitch these to the hearts at the ends of the garland. Sew a mother-of-pearl button over the stitched ribbons at the ends of the garland to finish.

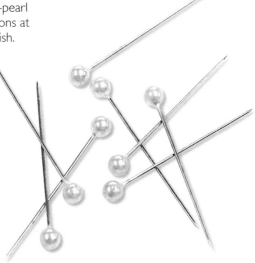

Linen burlap (hessian) with wired edges is a great material for making a wreath. Here it has been used to create a simple fabric wreath that is trimmed with a decorative linen flower and velvet ribbon leaves.

gathered
burlap wreath

materials

Paper and pencil
(for the petal template)

Scissors

Scraps of gray linen burlap
(for the decorative flower)

Pins

Sewing machine

Needle and thread

Mother-of-pearl button

Pliers

Circular wire wreath, 10in
(25cm) in diameter

40in (1m) wired burlap
ribbon, 2in (5cm) wide

White duct tape

Hot glue gun (or all-
purpose glue)

25in (65cm) velvet ribbon,
½in (1cm) wide, for the
hanging loop and leaves

1 To make the decorative flower, use the template on page 123 to trace a petal motif onto the piece of paper with the pencil, and cut out with the scissors. Fold a piece of linen burlap in half and pin the petal template to the fabric. Cut out a total of 10 petal shapes from the fabric in order to make five petals.

2 With right sides facing, use the sewing machine to stitch around the curved edges of the petal, leaving the straight side at the bottom open. Trim and notch the curved edges of the fabric using the scissors and turn right side out. Fold the sides of the petal toward the inside and stitch in place by hand. Repeat for all five petals.

3 Using small whip stitches, hand-stitch the five petals together to form the flower. Fasten off your sewing securely when you have finished.

4 Sew a mother-of-pearl button to the center of the flower by hand in order to cover up the stitches.

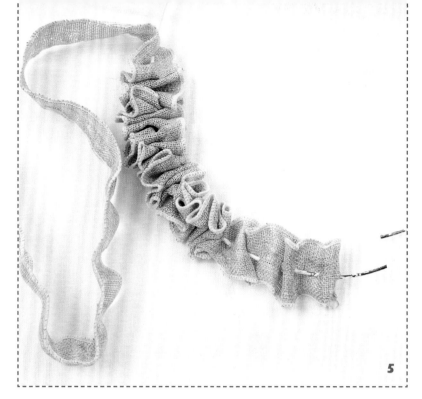

5 Use the pliers to cut the wire wreath open in one place so you can thread the burlap ribbon onto the wreath. Push the wire through the open weave of the ribbon at intervals of approximately ¾in (2cm). Push the ribbon along the wire wreath to form a neatly gathered row.

6 Continue to thread the burlap ribbon onto the wreath until you have used up all the ribbon. Gently tease the burlap so that the gathering is distributed evenly around the circular shape.

7 Cut a short length of duct tape and use this to stick the ends of the wire wreath back together. Wrap the tape around the wreath several times to keep it securely together.

8 Use glue or a hot glue gun to stick the decorative flower to the top of the wreath (the flower will cover the raw ends of the ribbon leaves). Cut four pieces of velvet ribbon, approximately 3in (8cm) in length, and fold them in half. Glue the ends of each of the ribbons together and stick these ribbon leaves behind the petals of the flower. Cut another piece of velvet ribbon, approximately 12in (30cm) in length, and thread this through the back of the wreath to form the hanging loop.

Use the heart design cards from a pack of playing cards mixed with painted wooden hearts to create this striking garland. You could also use the whole pack of cards to create a fun garland for a child's bedroom.

valentine's playing card garland

materials

Pack of playing cards

Wooden hearts

Paintbrush

Red acrylic paint

Drill with a fine drill bit

Hole punch

4¼yd (4m) red ribbon, ½in (1cm) wide

Red-and-white butcher's twine

Thick needle (optional)

Scissors

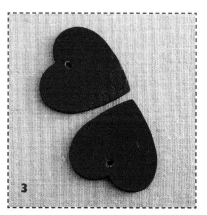

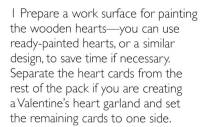

1 Prepare a work surface for painting the wooden hearts—you can use ready-painted hearts, or a similar design, to save time if necessary. Separate the heart cards from the rest of the pack if you are creating a Valentine's heart garland and set the remaining cards to one side.

2 Use the paintbrush to apply a coat of red paint to both sides and the edges of each wooden heart, and let dry completely. Apply a further coat of paint if better coverage is required, and let dry thoroughly.

3 Use the drill and a fine drill bit to make a small hole at the top of each wooden heart. Drill from the right side to the back to ensure the hole is smooth and the rough drilled edge will be at the back.

4 Use the hole punch to make two holes at the top of the heart cards, approximately ½in (1cm) from each edge. Repeat the process for each card.

5 Cut two lengths of ribbon, about 3in (8cm) long, for each playing card. Thread the lengths of ribbon through the punched holes and tie in a knot. Repeat for the other playing cards.

6 Cut a length of butcher's twine, measuring approximately 3in (8cm), for each wooden heart, and thread through the drilled hole. You may find it easier to use a thick needle to push the twine through the hole. Tie in a knot.

7 Cut a length of ribbon, about 1½yd (1.5m) long, or to the required length for your garland. Tie the first playing card to the ribbon, approximately 8in (20cm) from the end to allow for the hanging loop. Tie the ribbon firmly in a knot so that it will stay in position.

8 Tie a wooden heart to the ribbon, about 4in (10cm) along from the playing card, and tie firmly in a knot. Trim the ends of the butcher's twine using the scissors. Repeat the process along the length of the ribbon, alternating the heart playing cards and wooden hearts as you go. Tie a hanging loop at the ends of the ribbon to finish.

5

6

7

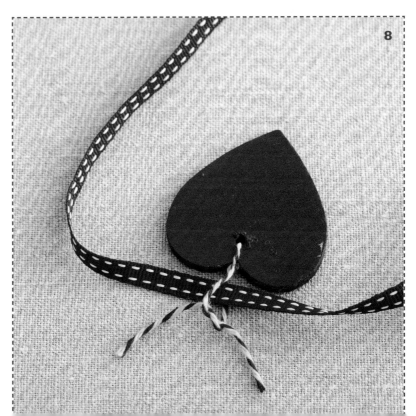

8

beach hut garland

This cute and colorful garland is made from felt beach huts and painted metal buckets—it would make a great addition to a child's bedroom or perhaps a seaside retreat.

materials

Paper and pencil (for the templates)

Scissors

Sheets of felt in three different colors (1 sheet makes two beach houses)

Pins

Needle

Embroidery floss (thread) in two contrasting colors

Red and blue gingham or striped fabric (for the door shapes)

1 button in a contrasting color (for each beach hut)

2¾yd (2.5m) red ribbon, ½in (1cm) wide

Miniature metal buckets

Red and blue acrylic paint

Paintbrush

1 Using the templates on page 123, trace the beach hut and door shapes onto a piece of paper with the pencil and cut them out with the scissors. Fold the first sheet of felt in half and pin the beach hut template to the fabric. Cut out the shape with the scissors. (Five beach huts were made for this garland, but the number needed will depend on the length of garland you are making.)

2 Place two of the felt shapes together, choosing a contrasting color for the back. Using embroidery floss (thread) in a contrasting color, start working blanket stitch around the edges of the hut. Continue until all of the edges have been stitched together. Repeat until you have the required number of beach huts.

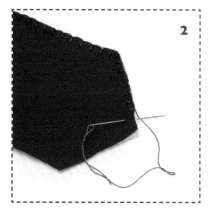

3 Pin the door template to the blue and red gingham or striped fabric and cut out the same number of doors as you have beach huts. Carefully pull away the strands of thread around the raw fabric edges to create a frayed effect. Continue until the frayed edges are about ¼in (5mm) deep.

Try creating themed garlands for different rooms or occasions—perhaps a garland of colorful felt flowers for a bedroom or triangular bunting for an outdoor party

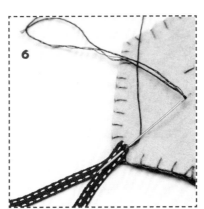

4 Place a door shape on the front of the beach hut and use running stitch to sew around all four edges, approximately ½in (1cm) in from the edge of the fabric. Repeat for the remaining beach huts.

5 Put a button in the center of the door shape and stitch by hand through all the layers of fabric. Repeat for each door shape.

6 Cut a length of ribbon, measuring approximately 4in (10cm), and fold it in half. Stitch the folded ribbon to the back of the beach hut at the top of the roof. Repeat for each beach hut.

7 Paint the metal buckets with blue and red paint, both inside and out, and let dry completely. Apply a further coat of paint to each bucket if better coverage is required and let dry. Cut a piece of ribbon, about 4in (10cm) long, and tie it to the handle of the bucket. Repeat for each bucket.

8 Cut a length of ribbon, approximately 1½yd (1.5m) long, and tie the beach huts and buckets to the ribbon, alternating them so that they are spaced about 5in (13cm) apart. Make sure they are tied securely so that they do not slip down the ribbon. Trim the ends of the ribbon on each bucket and beach hut diagonally to stop the ends fraying.

chapter three

Papercraft

paper
leaf wreath

This wreath is made from simple leaf shapes cut from old books—the yellowing page colors giving a vintage effect. It would look equally effective made with old musical sheet paper or even from old maps.

materials

Tracing paper, pencil, and piece of card (for the template)

Scissors

Old printed book or sheets of printed paper

Ready-woven wreath, approximately 10in (25cm) in diameter

Hot glue gun (or all-purpose glue)

12in (30cm) velvet ribbon, ½in (1cm) wide, for hanging

1 Using the template on page 125, trace the leaf motif onto the piece of paper with the pencil. Transfer the leaf motif to the piece of card and cut out the template with the scissors. Tear the printed pages from the book. Arrange the book pages—or sheets of printed paper if you are using these instead—in layers of about five to save time when cutting out the leaf shapes.

2 Use the pencil to draw around the leaf template onto the printed pages or sheets of paper, fitting as many leaves as you can onto one page or sheet.

3 Carefully cut out the leaf shapes and put the shapes to one side ready for sticking to the wreath.

4 Use glue or a hot glue gun to stick the leaf shapes to the wreath, overlapping them slightly to ensure the wreath is completely covered.

5 Continue to stick the leaf shapes to the wreath, using glue or the hot glue gun, until the wreath is covered on the top, sides, and inside.

6 Fold the remaining leaves in half lengthwise, running the edge of a ruler or pencil along the fold line to give a crisp edge.

7 Run a line of glue along the folded edge, and stick the folded leaves onto the wreath. Continue sticking until the wreath is completely covered with folded leaves.

8 Thread the velvet ribbon onto the wreath at the top and knot the ends to form a hanging loop. Trim the ends of the ribbon diagonally with the scissors to stop them fraying.

paper
daisy wreath

Delicate paper flowers and pretty daisies are combined in this simple wreath, which is beautifully finished with a dash of lime-green from the velvet ribbon.

materials

Scissors

White crepe paper

Hot glue gun (or all-purpose glue)

Wire wreath hoop, approximately 10in (25cm) in diameter

Small, ready-cut, white paper flowers

Plain white paper (for the daisy flowers)

Paper and pencil (for the template)

8 small fabric flowers (these were cut from a length of daisy braid)

16in (40cm) lime-green velvet ribbon, ½in (1cm) wide, for the hanging loop

Needle and thread

1 Cut the folded crepe paper into strips, measuring approximately ⅝in (1.5cm) in width. Cut about five strips through all the layers of folded crepe paper.

2 Use glue or a hot glue gun to apply a dab of glue to the edge of the wire wreath hoop and stick the end of the first strip of crepe paper to the hoop. Wrap the strip of crepe paper around the hoop and stick the strip to the hoop with another dab of glue when you reach the end. Keep wrapping the strips of crepe paper around the wire hoop until it is completely covered.

3 Use glue or the hot glue gun to stick the ready-cut paper flowers all around the wreath, slightly overlapping each one so that the wreath is covered completely.

4 To make the daisy flowers, cut out a piece of white paper, measuring 4 x 4in (10 x 10cm), and fold this into quarters. Using the template on page 124, trace off the daisy motif and cut out the template with the scissors.

5 Use the pencil to draw around the daisy template onto the piece of folded paper and cut out the shape with the scissors. Cut out a total of eight daisy flower shapes for the wreath and unfold them carefully.

6 Use glue or the hot glue gun to stick a fabric flower to the center of each daisy flower shape, and let the glue dry.

7 Use glue or the hot glue gun to stick the eight daisy flowers at equal distances around the wreath, and let the glue dry or cool completely.

8 Tie the velvet ribbon securely to the top of the wire hoop and stitch the ends of the ribbon together with the needle and thread to form a hanging loop.

tissue tassel and pompom garland

Made with tissue paper in colorful shades, this fun garland combines tassels with large pompoms to create the perfect decoration for any party or festive occasion.

materials

Pencil

Scissors

Ribbon (for suspending the tassels and pompoms)

For a tissue paper tassel:
1 sheet of tissue paper

12in (30cm) ruler

4in (10cm) silver ribbon, ¼in (5mm) wide

For a tissue paper pompom:
12 sheets of tissue paper

12in (30cm) silver ribbon, ¼in (5mm) wide

1 To make a tassel, fold the piece of tissue paper in half and press flat. Use the ruler to draw lines with the pencil on the tissue paper, approximately ⅝in (1.5cm) apart and 4in (10cm) from the folded edge. Carefully cut slits in the paper using the scissors.

2 Gently unfold the piece of tissue paper and lay it flat on a table. Begin to roll the tissue paper into a tube shape, teasing the fringed edges outward as you roll.

3 Once the tissue paper is rolled into a tube shape, fold it in half, and then twist the central section two or three times.

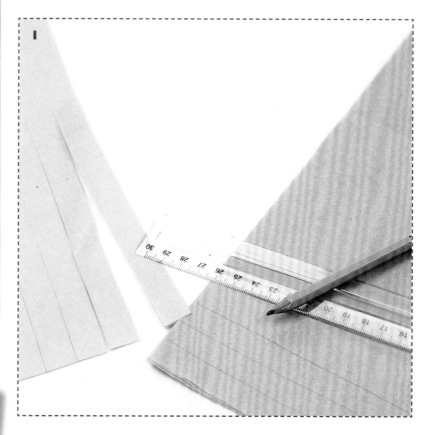

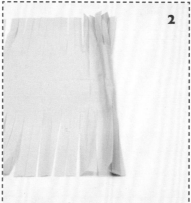

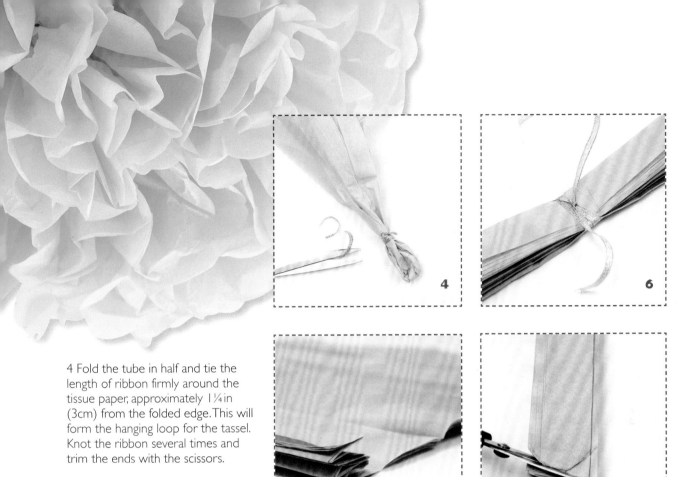

4 Fold the tube in half and tie the length of ribbon firmly around the tissue paper, approximately 1¼in (3cm) from the folded edge. This will form the hanging loop for the tassel. Knot the ribbon several times and trim the ends with the scissors.

5 To make a pompom, lay the 12 sheets of tissue paper on top of each other and make concertina-style folds, approximately 1in (2.5cm) wide, along the shorter edge of the paper.

6 Once all the tissue paper has been pleated, fold it in half to find the central point. Tie the length of ribbon around this point several times and knot securely. The long ends of the ribbon will be used to hang the pompom.

7 Use the pencil to draw a curved shape at both ends of the length of pleated tissue paper. Use the scissors to cut out the curved shape.

8 Carefully begin opening up the layers of tissue paper to create the pompom shape. Separate each layer and puff up the paper very gently, as tissue paper is easily torn. Repeat for the other side of the pompom.

9 Once you have made all of the pompoms and tassels, string them onto a long length of ribbon to create the finished garland. Hang from a ceiling or along a wall.

paper flower wreath

This delicate floral wreath is constructed from three-dimensional flowers made with vintage-style paper and finished with decorative buttons.

materials

Paper and pencil (for the flower templates)

Scissors

Floral paper or book of floral scrapbook paper

Hot glue gun (or all-purpose glue)

Colored buttons

Wire wreath hoop, approximately 10in (25cm) in diameter

16in (40cm) ribbon, ½in (1cm) wide, for the hanging loop

1 Using the templates on page 126, trace the three motifs onto a piece of paper with the pencil and cut them out. There are two flower designs, so you can mix and match them as you wish. To make the first design, fold a sheet of floral paper into quarters and place the larger flower template against the folded edges. Trace the flower onto the paper and cut out with scissors.

2 To create the central petals of the first flower design, trace the smaller flower template onto the floral paper and cut out with scissors. Fold the shape into quarters to give it a three-dimensional effect.

3 Unfold the larger flower shape and press it flat so that you will be able to stick the smaller flower shape to the center. Use glue or a hot glue gun to stick the smaller flower to the center of the larger flower.

Give this striking wreath
a festive twist by using
sheets of holiday gift wrap
or greetings cards covered
with fun Christmas motifs

4 To make the second flower design, you will need to cut out four heart shapes using the template you made in Step 1. Fold the floral paper in half, align the straight edge of the template with the folded paper edge, and draw around the heart shape. Cut out the heart with scissors and then cut a small eye-shape in the center of the fold in the paper.

5 Unfold the four heart shapes and use glue or a hot glue gun to stick them together at the central base point to create a flower.

6 Use glue or a hot glue gun to stick a colored button to the center of each flower and let the glue dry or cool.

7 Stick all of the paper flowers to the wreath hoop using glue or a hot glue gun. You will need quite a lot of glue to do this. Turn the wire wreath onto its reverse side and apply glue along the line of the wreath to keep the flowers firmly in place.

8 Thread the ribbon through the wire wreath hoop at the top and tie a small neat knot to form the hanging loop.

top tip

To add sparkle and shine to the wreath, use a large sequin to decorate the center of each paper flower instead of a colored button.

4

5

7

6

8

This fun paper garland is made with simple stars cut from decorative paper—you could also try using old comic books or maps for a different look.

paper star garland

materials

Paper, pencil, and piece of card (for the star template)

Scissors

Sheets of decorative paper

Thick needle

Butcher's twine in red and green

Hot glue gun (if required)

1 Using the template on page 125, trace the star motif onto the piece of paper with the pencil and then transfer the motif to the piece of card. Mark the small dots on the star template to show where the stitching will be done. Cut out the star template with the scissors.

2 Draw around the star template on the sheets of decorative paper and cut out with scissors. You will need approximately 25 stars to create the garland shown here.

3 Use the pencil to mark the dots on the front of the star where the hand-stitching will be done. Repeat for all the paper stars.

4 Thread the needle with a length of butcher's twine and knot the end. Begin stitching from one pencil dot mark to the opposite dot on the front of the star.

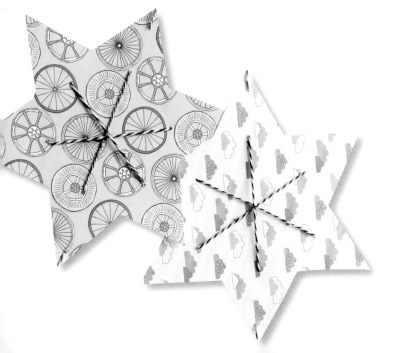

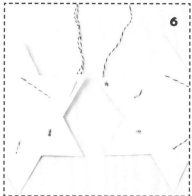

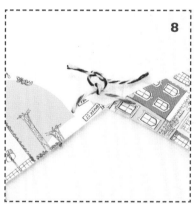

5 Repeat the stitching for all six of the pencil marks until you have created a stitched star design in the center of the paper star. Fasten off the stitching at the back of the star —you may find it easier to apply a blob of glue with a hot glue gun to the end of the butcher's twine rather than fastening off the stitching. Repeat for all the paper stars, using a mixture of red and green twine.

6 Push the threaded needle through one of the points of the first star, with the knot on the wrong side of the paper, and pull the butcher's twine through gently. Push the needle through the point of the next paper star.

7 Leave a length of butcher's twine, measuring approximately 1¼in (3cm), and knot the end at the back of the star. Trim the end of the twine with scissors. Repeat for all the paper stars so that they form a hanging garland.

8 Cut a short length of butcher's twine, measuring approximately 3in (8cm), and tie this to the middle of the twine joining each of the stars. Make a knot and trim the ends of the twine with the scissors, leaving about ¾in (2cm) on either side to finish.

If you are decorating a child's bedroom, choose paper decorated with their favorite cartoon characters or colorful patterns

paper chain garland

Make these colorful paper chains using two shades of pink paper and a delicate, lace-effect paper punch—you could also try making the garland in all-white to create a perfect wedding decoration.

materials

Ruler

Pencil

Letter size (A4) sheets of paper in pale and bright pink

Scissors

Decorative paper punch

Hot glue gun (or all-purpose glue) or a stapler

1 Use the ruler and pencil to mark out spaces, 2in (5cm) wide, along the longer side of the sheets of paper. (Each paper chain measures approximately 8½in /20cm in length, which is the width of the paper.)

2 Use the scissors to cut out the 2in (5cm) wide strips of paper and put these to one side. You will need to cut around 30 to 40 strips of paper to create a full garland.

3 Place the paper punch about ½in (1cm) in at one end of the first strip of paper and make the first punched design.

4 Move the paper punch along, match the pattern as shown on the paper punch, and make the next punched design. Repeat along the length of the paper chain.

Bring seasonal cheer to your home by making the paper chains with red, green, and white paper for the holidays

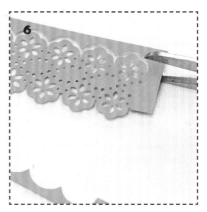

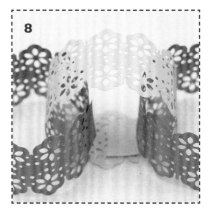

5 Move the paper punch to the other side of the paper chain and start punching the design along this side. Repeat until the whole paper chain is punched with the design leaving about ½in (1cm) at the end for the tab.

6 Trim the ends of the paper chain with the scissors to create a tab so that you will be able to glue the chains together. Repeat at both ends of each paper chain.

7 Use glue or a hot glue gun to join together the two ends of the first paper chain. You may find it quicker to use a stapler if you are making a large number of paper chains, but remember that the staples may show when the garland is suspended.

8 Thread the next paper chain through the first paper chain and join the ends together to form the first link of the garland. Repeat until all the paper chains are joined together and hang the finished garland as desired.

top tip

Rather than cutting a tab at the ends of each paper chain to glue them together, simply fold the chains to form a loop and glue the ends in place, overlapping them by about ½in (1cm).

chapter four

mixed media

beachcomber's garland

This simple garland is made from coarse rope and a selection of shells, starfish, and fish motifs. It would look great hanging outdoors or in a bathroom setting.

materials

Paper-covered florist's wire

28in (70cm) coarse rope, approximately ⅝in (1.5cm) in diameter

Selection of shells (pre-drilled), starfish, and other fish motifs

Drill with a very fine drill bit (optional)

Masking tape (optional)

Approximately 3¼yd (3m) fine wire

Hot glue gun (if required)

Pliers

1 Wrap the florist's wire around one end of the rope, starting about ¾in (2cm) in from the end. Twist the end of the wire several times to ensure it is firmly attached.

2 Continue to wrap the florist's wire around the end of the rope and then form a loop for hanging, before twisting the ends of the wire securely. Continue to wrap wire around the rope, as this will keep the hanging loop in place. Repeat the process for the other end of the rope.

3 If you cannot find pre-drilled shells, use a very fine drill bit to carefully drill a hole in each shell. You may find it easier to place a small piece of masking tape on the shell to stop the bit slipping as you drill. Once you have drilled the hole, thread the shell with a piece of fine wire, about 8in (20cm) in length, and neatly twist one end to keep it in place.

4 To make a hanging loop for the starfish, wrap an 8in (20cm) length of fine wire around one of the legs five or six times and then twist the ends of the wire. (You may wish to apply a blob of glue with a hot glue gun to the back of the wire to ensure it is securely fixed.)

5 Use short lengths of fine wire to attach the fish motifs to the rope and twist the ends several times to keep them in position. Trim the ends of the wire using the pliers.

6 To finish the garland, hang the shells and starfish at equal distances along the rope using short lengths of fine wire. Twist the ends of the wire several times to keep them in place as before. Trim the ends of the wire using the pliers.

This charming garland is made with sprayed pine cones and paper birds that have delicate, pleated tissue-paper wings—this makes the perfect alternative to a Christmas tree if you lack space in your home.

pine cone and bird garland

materials

Paper and pencil
(for the template)

Scissors

Gold and silver card

Gold and silver tissue paper

Sharp knife

Thick needle and fine string (for threading the birds)

Natural pine cones

Silver spray paint

Florist's wire

2yd (2m) natural string

Small natural wired pine cones

1 Using the template on page 123, trace the bird motif onto the piece of paper with the pencil and cut out with the scissors. Transfer the bird motif to the gold and silver card and cut out the shape with scissors. Cut out approximately five birds in each color.

2 Cut out a piece of tissue paper, measuring 4 x 10in (10 x 25cm), and fold concertina-style pleats, each approximately ¾in (2cm) wide, along the longer side of the paper. Press the pleats flat using the edge of a ruler or pencil.

3 Use a sharp knife or blade to cut a slit in the middle of the birds (as shown on the template). This is the space through which you will insert the pleated tissue-paper wings.

4 Fold the pleated tissue paper in half and carefully push it through the slit in the bird. Fluff out the wings carefully so that they look full. Repeat for all five birds.

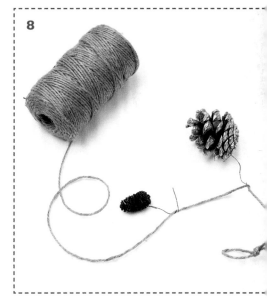

5 Thread the fine string onto the thick needle and pierce the birds, using the photograph above as a guide to where to pierce the hole. Pull the string through and cut it to make a hanging loop that measures approximately 4in (10cm) in length. Knot the ends of the string to form the hanging loop.

6 Spray the larger natural pine cones with a fine layer of silver paint—make sure you do this either outdoors or in a well-ventilated space. Allow the silver paint to dry completely. Apply a further coat of silver paint if required.

7 Cut a length of florist's wire, approximately 8in (20cm) in length, and wrap this around the base of a pine cone, twisting the ends together. Wire all of the silver-sprayed pine cones in the same way.

8 Tie a silver-sprayed pine cone to one end of the string and twist the ends around the string to keep it in place. Attach a small wired pine cone, about 4in (10cm) further along the string. Attach the next silver-sprayed pine cone to the string, followed by another small wired pine cone, repeating the process until you have the required length of garland. String from twigs, and hang the gold and silver birds from the branches to finish.

starfish
driftwood wreath

The perfect addition for any bathroom, this simple wreath is made from a square wire frame and decorated with pieces of driftwood, shells, and starfish.

materials

Fine twigs

Wire wreath (with three frames), approximately 12in (30cm) square

Fine wire

Pliers

40–45 pieces of driftwood, approximately 2in (5cm) in length

Paper-covered florist's wire

Hot glue gun (or all-purpose glue)

1 large starfish

Selection of small starfish and shells

8in (20cm) string (for the hanging loop)

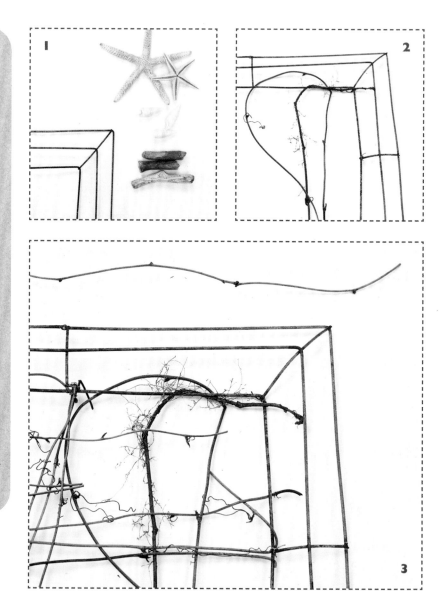

1 Soak the fine twigs in a bowl of water or in the kitchen sink—this will help to soften them so they can be wrapped easily around the center of the wire wreath.

2 Start by wrapping one length of the damp twigs around the inner frame of the wire wreath. Use a short length of fine wire to keep it in place if required.

3 Continue wrapping damp twigs around and across the inner frame of the wreath, running them horizontally and vertically in order to create a delicate criss-cross pattern. Use short lengths of fine wire to hold the ends of the twigs in place if necessary. Trim the ends of the wire with the pliers.

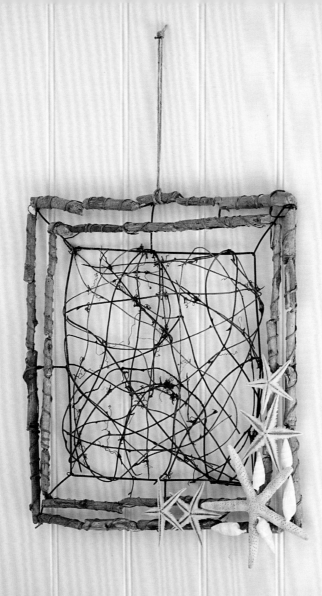

Create a rustic woodland theme by replacing the pieces of driftwood around the frames with long pine cones and then decorating the wreath with ears of corn, dried seedpods, and autumn leaves

4 Place the first piece of driftwood on the outer corner of the wire wreath. Wrap a length of paper-covered florist's wire around the driftwood and secure in place by twisting the wire several times. Continue to wrap the wire around the piece of driftwood to keep it in position. (You may wish to apply a layer of glue with a hot glue gun to the back of the pieces of driftwood to make them more secure. Let the glue cool completely.)

5 Place the next piece of driftwood on the wreath and wrap florist's wire around it as before. If required, apply glue using the hot glue gun to the back of the driftwood pieces to keep them in position.

6 Continue attaching pieces of driftwood to the outer frame of the wreath and then attach driftwood to the middle frame in the same way, securing the ends of the florist's wire by twisting them together several times.

7 Using glue or a hot glue gun, stick the large starfish, small starfish, and shells to one corner of the wire wreath, and allow the glue to cool.

8 Wrap the piece of string around the center of the top of the wreath and knot tightly to create a hanging loop.

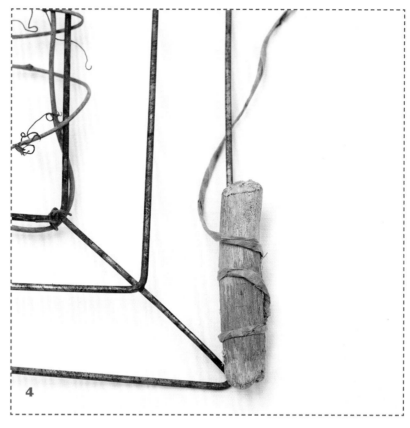

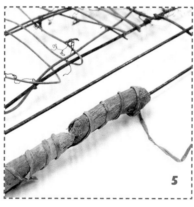

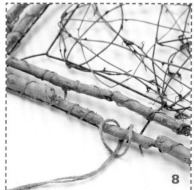

top tip

If you don't have any fine twigs to hand, use some coarse string or natural-colored yarn to create the woven effect in the central part of the wreath.

textured rope
shell wreath

Make this bold, nautical-inspired wreath from a simple polystyrene hoop, which is tightly wrapped with rope and then decorated with shells arranged in a flower shape.

materials

Rope

Scissors

Polystyrene hoop, approximately 12in (30cm) in diameter

Hot glue gun (or all-purpose glue)

Selection of decorative shells

String (for the hanging loop)

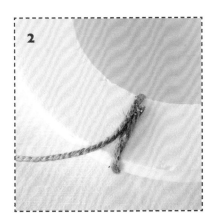

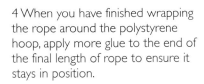

1 Cut the rope into lengths, each measuring approximately 20in (50cm), using the scissors. This will make it easier to wrap the rope around the polystyrene hoop and also stop the rope from getting tangled.

2 Place the first length of rope around the back of the polystyrene hoop and wrap it once around the hoop. Use glue or a hot glue gun to join the two pieces of rope together, making sure that they are glued as tightly as possible so that the polystyrene does not show through.

3 Continue to wrap the lengths of rope around the hoop, pulling firmly so that the ropes are tightly bound. Slightly overlap each length of rope after every four or five wraps, so that it covers the hoop completely. Continue to apply glue to the back of the hoop to keep the lengths of rope in place.

4 When you have finished wrapping the rope around the polystyrene hoop, apply more glue to the end of the final length of rope to ensure it stays in position.

5 Cut a length of string, approximately 10in (25cm) in length, and tie it around the top of the rope wreath. Knot the ends of the string to form a hanging loop.

6 Use glue or the hot glue to stick the shells to one side of the rope hoop. They have been arranged in a flower shape here, but you could use a selection of shells and small starfish to create a different look if you wish.

Make a break with tradition and create this driftwood wreath in an unusual triangular shape and decorate it with handmade metal boats, which are easy to make using punched tin sheeting.

triangular tin boat wreath

1 Paint the driftwood twigs with blue paint and let dry completely. Apply a second coat of paint for better coverage if required. Let dry before making up the wreath.

2 Lay the three driftwood twigs on a flat surface and overlay them at the ends to form a triangular shape. Apply a dab of glue, using the hot glue gun if you have one, to each twig so that they are stuck together before tying them with string. Wrap a piece of string around each corner of the wreath so the twigs are firmly tied together. Leave one end of the string untied at each corner so you can attach the two side boats.

3 Using the template on page 124, trace the boat motif onto a piece of paper using the pencil and cut out with the scissors. Use the pencil to draw around the boat motif onto the back of the tin metal sheeting

4 Carefully cut out the boat motifs with the scissors. Four tin boats were used here, but you could add more, if you wish, or perhaps cut out some different seashore-themed shapes such as shells, from the tin sheeting.

5 Turn the boats to the wrong side and place them on a soft flat surface such as a dish towel or piece of cloth. Use the fine stick (or the end of the paintbrush) to make punched holes around the edges of each boat and two rows down the center.

6 Use the punch or sharp-nosed pliers (or similar) to pierce a hole in the top of each boat in the middle of the triangular sail section—this is where you will thread the string for hanging the boat.

7 Using the string left from binding the pieces of driftwood, cut a piece of string, approximately 6in (15cm) in length, and thread this through the hole at the top of the first tin boat. Tie a knot at one end of the string and then trim the end with the scissors. Gently pull the string though the hole and tie the boat to the wreath in the center of the bottom section.

8 Thread the three remaining tin boats with string in the same way, tying a knot at one end of the string and trimming it with the scissors. Using the ends of the pieces of string you left in Step 2, tie a tin boat to the bottom corners of the triangle. Tie the fourth boat to the center top of the triangle so that it hangs in the middle of the triangular wreath. Thread a piece of string through the top of the wreath and knot securely to form a hanging loop.

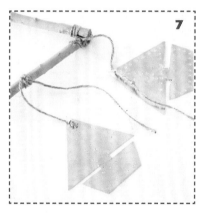

cloud and raindrop mobile

This cute mobile is made from cloud-shaped felt motifs decorated with twinkling blue glass beads, which will catch the light if you hang the mobile in a window.

materials

Paper and pencil (for the cloud template)

Scissors

1 sheet of white felt (for each cloud shape)

Needle

White embroidery floss (thread)

Polyester fiber filling

Blue glass beads (for the raindrop decorations)

Wooden embroidery hoop, 6in (15cm) in diameter

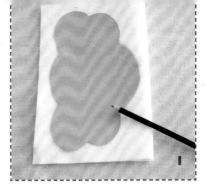

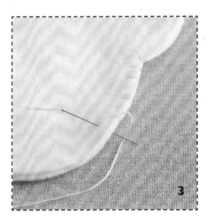

1 Using the template on page 126, trace the cloud motif onto a piece of paper with the pencil and cut out with the scissors. Fold the first sheet of felt in half and draw around the cloud template with the pencil.

2 Carefully cut out the cloud shape with the scissors and repeat the process until you have the required number of clouds for your mobile.

3 Thread the needle with embroidery floss (thread) and begin working blanket stitch around the curved edges of the cloud shape. Continue to embroider around the shape, but leave an opening of about 3in (8cm) for inserting the filling.

4 Pull off small pieces of polyester fiber filling and gently push them into the cloud shape. You may find it easier to use the end of a pencil to

do this to ensure the fiber fills out the curved shapes of the cloud.

5 Once you have filled the cloud shape, finish the blanket stitching so that the opening is completely closed and then fasten off your stitching. Repeat for each cloud shape.

6 Cut a length of embroidery floss (thread) measuring approximately 12in (30cm). Thread the first bead onto one end of the thread and knot the thread several times so the bead cannot slip off. Trim the end of the thread with scissors. Tie another knot, about 2in (5cm) along from the first bead, so that the second bead will not slip off. Thread the second bead onto the thread. Repeat for the third bead. Repeat this process until you have three lengths of beads for each cloud shape. For added interest, some of the lengths for the cloud shapes can be threaded with two beads instead of three.

7 Take one of the lengths of beads, thread the end of the embroidery floss (thread) onto the needle, and stitch the beads to a curved edge of the cloud shape. Repeat this process until you have stitched three lengths of beads to each cloud shape.

8 Cut another three lengths of embroidery floss (thread), each measuring about 12in (30cm). Thread a length of embroidery floss (thread) onto the needle and stitch it to the top center of the first cloud shape. Attach the other end of the thread to the embroidery hoop, wrapping it around several times. Knot the end of the thread and trim the ends with scissors. Repeat this for each cloud shape, making sure these are fixed at equally spaced points around the hoop. Tie three more lengths of embroidery floss (thread) to the hoop in the gaps between the first three lengths, and knot securely. Gather together the tops of the threads and tie in a knot ready for hanging.

rope and shell candle wreath

Create these simple candle wreaths using lengths of rope and then decorate them with pretty white shells. Group the candle wreaths in rows and pop a glass jar with a tea-light candle inside each one for a great summer table setting idea.

materials

12in (30cm) rope (for each rope wreath)

Scissors or sharp knife

Hot glue gun (or all-purpose glue)

Selection of seashells or tiny starfish (to decorate)

Glass jars and tea-light candles

1 You will need to cut a length of rope measuring 12in (30cm) for each wreath. If the rope is very strong, you may find it easier to cut the rope with a sharp knife rather than scissors. Use glue, or apply some glue with a hot glue gun, to both ends of the rope to stop them fraying and allow the glue to dry or cool.

2 Bend the length of rope into a circular shape, apply more glue to each end, and press the ends together firmly. Hold the ends together until the glue has completely dried or cooled.

3 Apply glue, using the hot glue gun if you have one, to the underside of the first shell and stick it to the top of the rope wreath. Let the glue dry or cool. You could also decorate the rope with some tiny starfish, if you wish.

4 Continue to stick shells to the top of the rope wreath, using glue or the hot glue gun, until the wreath is completely covered. Use a glass jar and tea-light candle to make a pretty votive and tie lengths of string around the rim of the jar to finish.

clay bell and vintage bell garland

This delightful garland is made using miniature vintage cow bells and gold-painted bells fashioned from clay. The bells are strung along a piece of rope to make a wonderful addition to a country-style setting.

materials

Air-dry clay

Rolling pin

Bell-shaped cookie cutter

Spatula

Scissors

Drinking straw

Paintbrush

Gold acrylic paint

String

1½yd (1.2m) ribbon, ½in (1cm) wide (for approximately 10 cow bells)

10 miniature vintage cow bells (or more for a longer garland)

2yd (2m) rope

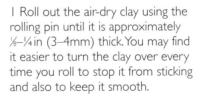

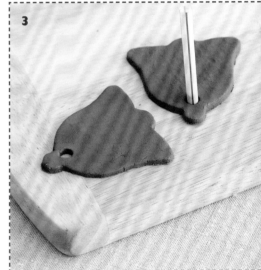

1 Roll out the air-dry clay using the rolling pin until it is approximately ⅛–¼in (3–4mm) thick. You may find it easier to turn the clay over every time you roll to stop it from sticking and also to keep it smooth.

2 Press the bell-shaped cookie cutter firmly into the clay. Use a spatula to lift the bell shape carefully from the board and lay it flat. Repeat the process until you have approximately 8 bell shapes, or more depending on the length of garland you wish to make.

3 Use the scissors to cut the drinking straw down to approximately 2in (5cm) in length, and press the end into the top of the bell shape to create a hole for the hanging loop. Repeat for each bell shape. Lay the bell shapes on a piece of kitchen towel (or similar) and let dry according to the manufacturer's instructions.

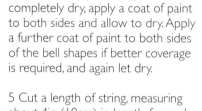

4 When the clay bell shapes are completely dry, apply a coat of paint to both sides and allow to dry. Apply a further coat of paint to both sides of the bell shapes if better coverage is required, and again let dry.

5 Cut a length of string, measuring about 4in (10cm) in length, for each bell shape. Thread the string through the hole in the bell shape and tie the ends, as shown. Repeat for each bell shape.

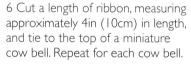

6 Cut a length of ribbon, measuring approximately 4in (10cm) in length, and tie to the top of a miniature cow bell. Repeat for each cow bell.

7 Tie the ribbon on the first cow bell to the rope, approximately 8in (20cm) in from one end, and pull tightly so that the bell stays firmly in place. Trim the ends of the ribbon diagonally using the scissors to prevent the ends fraying.

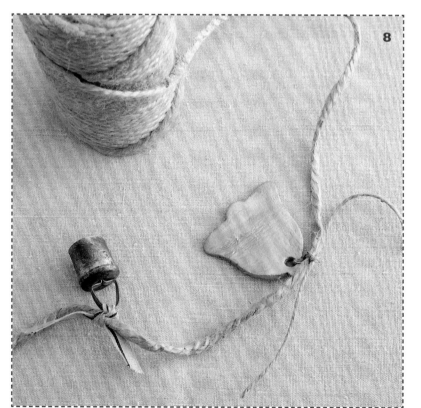

8 Tie a gold clay bell to the rope, about 4in (10cm) along from the cow bell, using the string you threaded through earlier. Knot the string tightly to keep the clay bell in place. Trim the ends of the string with the scissors. Repeat the process, tying the next cow bell about 4in (10cm) along from the clay bell. Repeat until the required length of garland has been made. Knot the ends of the rope to create hanging loops for stringing and displaying the garland.

tea-light votive garland

A delightful addition to any garden, this pretty garland is made from hand-decorated glass jars that are suspended along a rope.

materials

Glass jars (or recycled glass yogurt pots)

Detergent (for cleaning the glass jars or pots)

Three-dimensional fabric paint in a tube (or glass paint and a very fine paintbrush)

String

Scissors

Thin wire (for the handles)

Wire cutters

Pliers

Rope

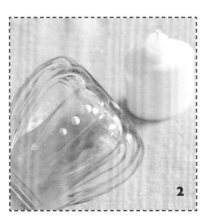

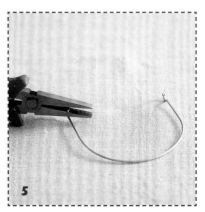

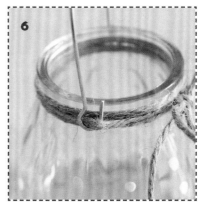

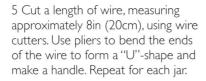

1 Wash the jars in soapy detergent to ensure they are clean and free from grease—this will create a key for the paint. Dry thoroughly.

2 Use the three-dimensional fabric paint, or glass paint and a paintbrush, to draw a row of tiny dots on one side of the jar.

3 Repeat the rows of dots around the whole of the jar and let dry. Repeat for each jar. The drying process can take several hours, but it's important to ensure the paint is completely dry before the next step.

4 Wrap the string around the neck of the jar two or three times, and tie in a bow. Cut the ends of the string. Repeat for each jar.

5 Cut a length of wire, measuring approximately 8in (20cm), using wire cutters. Use pliers to bend the ends of the wire to form a "U"-shape and make a handle. Repeat for each jar.

6 Hook the wire handle under one layer of the string tied around the neck of the jar and use pliers to pinch the wire together and hold it in place. Repeat on the other side to finish the handle. Repeat for each jar.

7 Cut a length of string, measuring approximately 6in (15cm), for each jar and tie to the top of the handle. Repeat for each jar.

8 Tie the string attached to the handle to the piece of rope, approximately 8in (20cm) in from the end to leave some rope for

creating the hanging loop. Pull the ends of the string tightly and tie in a knot so the jar is held in position. Trim the ends of the string. Repeat for each jar, spacing them evenly along the rope (about 8in/20cm apart). Tie the ends of the rope in a knot to form two hanging loops.

chapter five

holidays & special occasions

wire hanging wreath

This delicate wire wreath is bound with frosted pine picks and decorated with silvered candle clips and tiny pine cones. It looks simply lovely hanging above a table.

materials

Pliers

⅛in (3mm) wire (to form the circles)

White tape

Frosted pine picks

Fine wire (for wrapping the pine picks)

¹⁄₁₆in (1mm) wire (for hanging)

10 wired pine cones

Silver candle clips

White candles (to fit the clips)

1 Use the pliers to cut three lengths from the ⅛in (3mm) wire to form three circles measuring 12in (30cm), 10in (25cm), and 8in (20cm) in diameter, adding 8in (20cm) to each length for overlapping. Bend the wire round to form the three circles.

2 Cut short lengths of white tape and carefully wrap these around the wire to hold the circular shapes in place. I used three pieces of tape at equal intervals around each circle of wire.

3 Bend the frosted pine picks around the first circular wire shape and wrap fine wire around the picks to keep them in place. Repeat for each circle of wire.

4 Use the pliers to cut eight lengths of the ¹⁄₁₆in (1mm) wire, each measuring approximately 12in (30cm) in length. Fold the ends of four of the lengths of wire around the base of the larger wire circle by approximately ⅝in (1.5cm), spacing the wires at equal distances. Use the pliers to nip the wire ends so they fit securely to the wire circle.

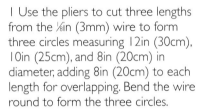

top tip

To give shiny candle clips a more aged and vintage look, soak them in a bowl of water containing a dissolved dishwasher tablet. This will give the clips a more matt effect.

5 Fold the top ends of the wire over the medium-sized wire circle by approximately ⅝in (1.5cm), spacing the wires at equal distances, and use the pliers to nip the wire ends to keep them in position as before.

6 Fold the remaining four lengths of wire over the medium-sized wire circle midway between the first set of wire loops. Use the pliers to nip the wire ends to keep them firmly in place. Repeat the process by folding the top ends of the wire over the smallest wire circle. Cut another four lengths of wire, measuring approximately 20in (50cm) in length, and fold these over the top of the smallest wire circle to create the hanging wire. Twist the ends to form a hook for hanging.

7 Attach the wired pine cones to the three circles, bending the wire around the circle wire several times to keep the cones in position.

8 Attach the candle clips to the lower and middle circles of wire. Cut the candles down in size if you think the flames will affect the wire above.

(Safety note: never leave lit candles unattended.)

leaf and berry
christmas wreath

This simple yet effective wreath is made with twigs and a combination of fresh foliage and artificial berries. The off-center position of the foliage gives this wreath a casual and less formal style.

materials

Selection of fine and thicker twigs

Fine wire

Pliers

Sprigs of fresh foliage, such as rosemary, weigela, and *Skimmia japonica* 'Kew Green'

Frosted red artificial berries or berry picks

Hot glue gun (or all-purpose glue)

Artificial ivy leaves

12in (30cm) red ribbon, ½in (1cm) wide, for hanging

Scissors

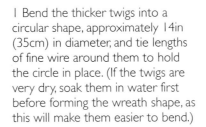

1 Bend the thicker twigs into a circular shape, approximately 14in (35cm) in diameter, and tie lengths of fine wire around them to hold the circle in place. (If the twigs are very dry, soak them in water first before forming the wreath shape, as this will make them easier to bend.)

2 Continue to bend and weave the twigs, twisting lengths of wire around them at regular intervals. Twist the wire several times to ensure the twigs are held firmly in position. Trim the wire ends with the pliers.

3 Start wrapping the finer twigs around the wreath on top of the thicker ones, using wire to hold them in place as before.

4 Continue to wrap the finer twigs around the wreath, but keep some of them looser with the ends unwired to give the wreath a less formal effect.

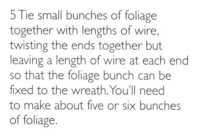

5 Tie small bunches of foliage together with lengths of wire, twisting the ends together but leaving a length of wire at each end so that the foliage bunch can be fixed to the wreath. You'll need to make about five or six bunches of foliage.

6 Use the wire to attach the foliage bunches to one side of the wreath, twisting the ends of the wire tightly around the twigs. Use the pliers to trim away the ends of the wire. Attach all the foliage bunches in this way.

7 Attach short lengths of wire to the artificial berries and fix them to the wreath on top of the foliage bunches. Use glue or a hot glue gun to stick some artificial ivy leaves to the wreath twigs.

8 Tie the length of ribbon to the top of the wreath and knot the ends to form a hanging loop. Trim the ends of the ribbon diagonally with the scissors to stop them fraying.

Replace the winter foliage and crimson berries with pretty meadow flowers such as *Centaurea cyanus* (cornflower) and *Leucantheum vulgare* (ox-eye daisy) to create an ephemeral summer display

This simple twig wreath is decorated with brightly colored Chinese lanterns and leaves, making it the perfect decoration for Hallowe'en or a Harvest Festival celebration.

hallowe'en wreath

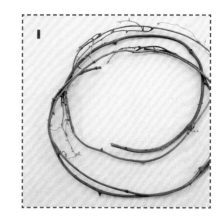

materials

Selection of fine and thicker twigs (for making the wreath framework)

Paper-covered florist's wire

Chinese lantern garland or some fresh *Physalis alkekengi* (Chinese lantern) flowers

Fresh red leaves (some *Acer palmatum*/Japanese maple leaves were used here)

39in (1m) linen (hessian) burlap ribbon, 2in (5cm) wide

Scissors

String (for the hanging loop)

1 Start bending the twigs to form a wreath shape, approximately 14in (35cm) in diameter. You will find this easier if you soak the twigs in water for a couple of hours first in order to soften them and make them easier to bend.

2 Use lengths of florist's wire to bind the twigs together and create the circular shape. Continue to bend the twigs to form the circular shape and bind them with florist's wire until the wreath is formed.

3 Wrap the Chinese lantern garland—or fresh Chinese lantern flowers if you are using these—around the wreath and keep in place using florist's wire.

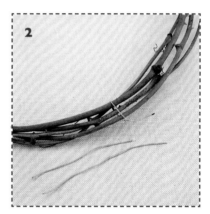

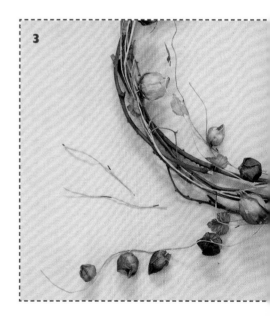

Echo the time of year by decorating the wreath with autumn leaves and seedheads, or perhaps with spiced orange slices and artificial berries

4 Take the Japanese maple leaves, wrap a small length of florist's wire around the base of the stems, and start attaching them to the wreath. Repeat around the whole wreath, ensuring the leaves are spaced out evenly.

5 Thread the burlap ribbon through one of the twigs at the top of the wreath and pull it through gently. Tie the ribbon in a bow and cut the ribbon ends diagonally using the scissors to prevent the fabric fraying.

6 Cut a length of string, measuring approximately 16in (40cm), and loop this through the ribbon at the top of the wreath. Pull the loop to fit and then knot the ends of the string to form the hanging loop.

top tip

Make this decoration more suitable for a fun-filled children's Hallowe'en party by decorating the wreath with a garland of Hallowe'en lanterns.

heart fairy light wreath

A simple, heart-shaped form fashioned out of thick wire can be wrapped with fairy lights to create a twinkling wreath that is perfect for the festive season.

materials

39in (1m) wire, approximately 17 gauge (1.2mm diameter)

Thin wire

Pliers

Thin florist's wire

Fairy lights

Red berry bunch, for decoration (optional)

10in (25cm) red ribbon, ½in (1cm) wide, for the hanging loop

Needle and thread

1 Fold the wire in half to form a V-shape and lay it flat. Fold the ends inward so they overlap and push them down toward the V-shape to form the top of the heart. Bend the wire so the ends overlap. Take a length of thin wire and wrap this around the thicker wire, twisting the ends several times to keep the shape in place. Trim the wire ends with pliers.

2 Use a length of florist's wire to attach one end of the lights to the heart, twisting the ends securely. Wrap the lights around the heart, attaching them with lengths of wire.

3 Continue to wrap the lights, fixing them in place with florist's wire, and wrapping them round again if necessary.

4 Attach a length of florist's wire to the berry bunch and fix this to the thicker wire at the top, twisting the ends to keep it in place.

5 Tie the ribbon to the center of the heart and stitch the ends together with the needle and thread to form a hanging loop.

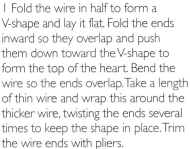

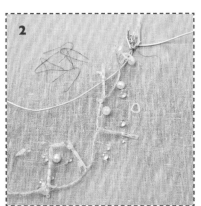

Replace the red berries with small
Christmas baubles or sleigh bells, and
use silver instead of scarlet ribbon,
to create a more sparkly effect

hanging ivy wreath

This simple wreath, with its glittering ivy leaf and red berry decorations, makes a great addition to any festive occasion when suspended by ribbons and hung low over a dining table.

materials

Paintbrush

White (PVA) glue

Swag of real or artificial ivy

White glitter

Pliers

Thin wire

Large wreath frame, approximately 16in (40cm) in diameter

4 red berry picks

6 lengths of ribbon, approximately 24in (60cm) long and ½in (1cm) wide

Needle and thread

Scissors

Hot glue gun (or all-purpose glue)

S hook (for hanging)

1 Use the paintbrush to apply a fine coat of white (PVA) glue to each ivy leaf and then sprinkle with glitter. Allow the glitter to dry completely before continuing.

2 Use the pliers to cut short lengths of thin wire, measuring approximately 4in (10cm). Start winding the ivy around the wreath frame.

3 Fix the end of the ivy swag securely by wrapping a length of wire around the frame several times and twisting the ends together. Trim the ends of the wire with the pliers. Continue wrapping the ivy around the frame and then twisting lengths of wire around the ivy and hoop at intervals of approximately 4in (10cm).

4 Use short lengths of wire to fix the berry picks at regular intervals around the frame. Twist the wire together several times and trim the ends with the pliers.

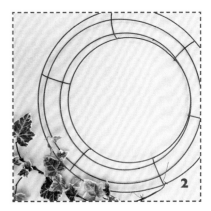

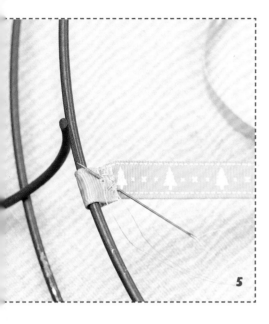

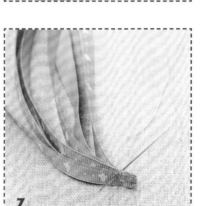

5 Fold the end of the first length of ribbon around the inner circle of the frame and stitch into position with the needle and thread. Sew the remaining five lengths of ribbon to the frame's inner circle at regular intervals.

6 Cut six small ivy leaves from the swag and use glue or a hot glue gun to stick one over each ribbon section to cover up the stitching.

7 Layer together the other end of the six ribbon lengths and stitch them securely with the needle and thread.

8 Fold the end of the stitched lengths of ribbon around the inside curve of the S hook and stitch together securely.

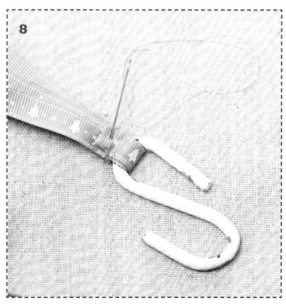

gold star wreath

Make a trio of gold star-shaped wreaths, perhaps in different sizes, to create a pretty festive display and finish the wreaths with miniature gold vintage bells tied simply with lengths of string.

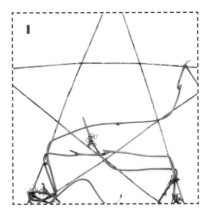

materials

Star-shaped metal wreath frame

Fine twigs

Fine florist's wire

Gold spray paint

Miniature gold bell

String

1 Lay the wreath frame on a flat surface and begin to bend the twigs gently around the frame. You will find it easier to work with the twigs if they have been soaked in water for a couple of hours first because this makes them more pliable and less likely to break.

2 Continue to bend the twigs around the wire frame, forming a criss-cross pattern, and use small lengths of florist's wire to fix them to the frame.

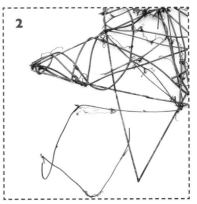

3 Apply a coat of gold spray paint to both sides of the finished wreath and leat dry. Apply a further coat of spray paint to both sides if better coverage is required, and leave to dry. (Safety note: it is important that you only use spray paint in a well-ventilated area or preferably outdoors due to the fumes.)

4 Cut a piece of string, approximately 8in (20cm) in length, and tie this to the top of the miniature bell. Thread the string through one of the points of the star and tie into a bow to finish. Thread a longer piece of string through the same point in order to hang and display the wreath.

Use metal wreath frames shaped as Christmas trees or snowflakes to create other festive scenes, spraying them silver instead of gold and suspending them with silver ribbon

This delicate wreath is made from slender stems of pussy willow, with soft, velvety flowers, and decorated with speckled eggs and fluffy feathers—making it perfect for a door or cupboard at Easter.

pussy willow
easter wreath

materials

Hand pruners (secateurs)

5 or 6 stems of pussy willow

Pliers

24in (60cm) copper wire

White tape

Florist's wire

Hot glue gun (or all-purpose glue)

Approximately 8–10 feathers

Small plastic eggs

Narrow ribbon, ½in (1cm) wide, for hanging the wreath

Scissors

1 Using the hand pruners (secateurs), cut off the thicker base stems of the pussy willow branches. This will make them easier to bend and form the wreath shape. Keep the pussy willow branches in water until they are needed so they will be damp and easier to work with.

2 Use the pliers to cut a piece of copper wire, measuring approximately 20in (50cm) in length. Bend the length of wire into a circular shape, with approximately ½in (1cm) overlapping at both ends so that you can tape them together. Cut a couple of pieces of white tape and use these to tape the ends of the wire together to form the circular wreath shape.

3 Take the first stem of pussy willow and twist a length of florist's wire around the stem to fix it to the circular wreath. Continue to twist the wire around the stem to start creating the wreath.

4 Continue to wrap the pussy willow stems around the wreath, overlapping them as you work so that none of the copper wire is showing. Twist the ends of the florist's wire several times to secure it in place.

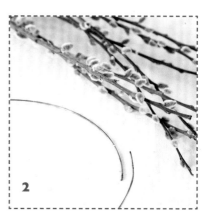

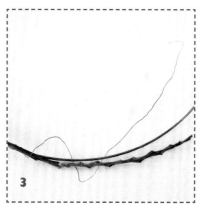

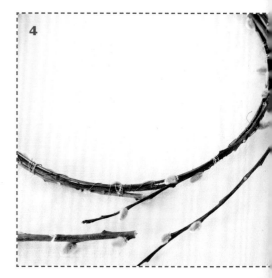

5 Wrap several lengths of florist's wire around the pussy willow stems to ensure they are securely fastened.

6 Use glue or a hot glue gun to fix approximately eight feathers to one side of the wreath. You can add more feathers if required all around the wreath for a more decorative effect.

7 Use glue or the hot glue gun to stick two small decorative eggs to the top of the feathers on the wreath. For a more realistic effect, you could use real quail's eggs once they have been blown.

8 Cut a piece of ribbon, measuring approximately 16in (40cm) in length, thread it through the top of the wreath, and tie firmly. Knot the ends of the ribbon to form a hanging loop. Trim the ends of the ribbon diagonally using the scissors to stop the ends fraying.

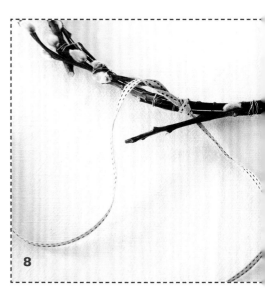

Create a more temporary display, perhaps for an Easter Day celebration, by decorating the wreath with pretty spring flowers such as daffodils and tulips

templates

Each template is printed at actual size. Before use, you can either trace the template or photocopy it. Once you have copied the template, cut it out using scissors and draw around it if you are using paper, or if you are using fabric, pin it to the fabric and cut around it.

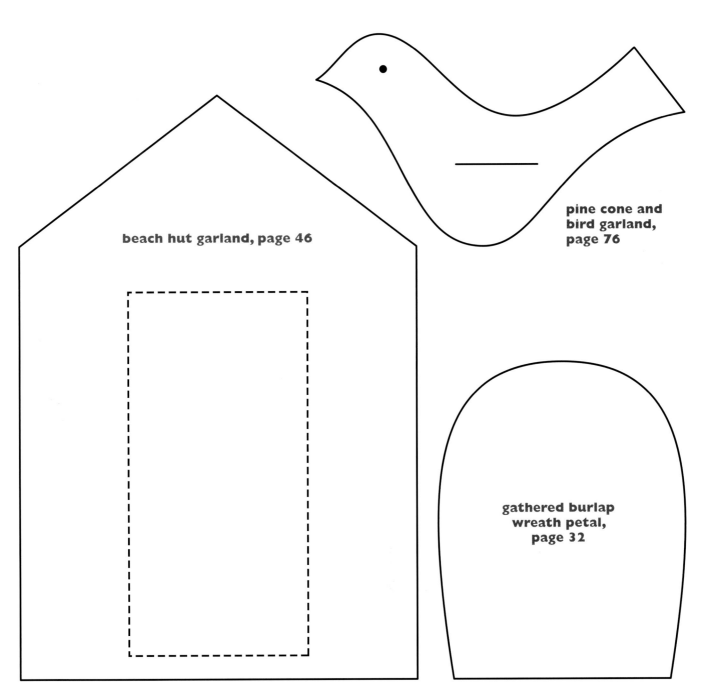

beach hut garland, page 46

pine cone and
bird garland,
page 76

gathered burlap
wreath petal,
page 32

templates continued

fabric heart
garland—medium
heart, page 34

triangular tin boat
wreath, page 86

paper daisy
wreath,
page 54

fabric heart
garland—small
heart, page 34

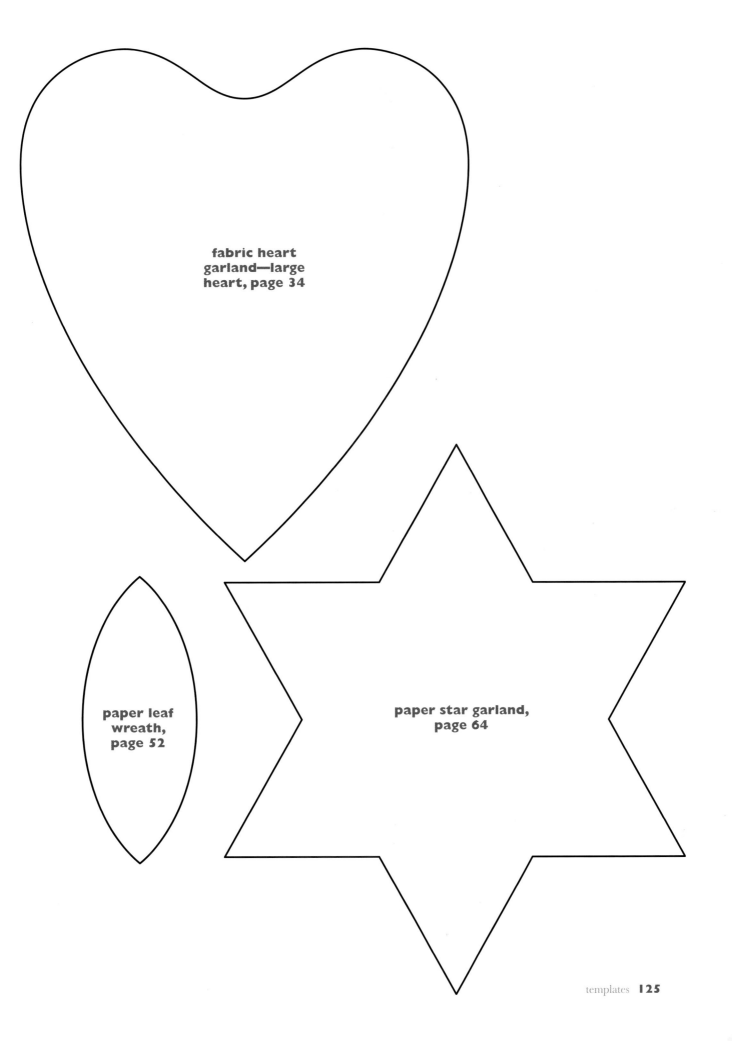

fabric heart
garland—large
heart, page 34

paper leaf
wreath,
page 52

paper star garland,
page 64

templates continued

cloud and raindrop
mobile, page 88

paper flower
wreath—heart,
page 60

paper flower
wreath—large
flower, page 60

paper flower
wreath—small
flower, page 60

suppliers

UNITED STATES

A. C. Moore
www.acmoore.com
Arts and crafts superstore stocking different papers, decorative beads, and stamps, as well as scrapbooking supplies.

Britex Fabrics
www.britexfabrics.com
Online supplier of excellent range of fabrics, buttons, lace, ribbons, notions.

Create for Less
www.createforless.com
Large selection of craft, needlework, and sewing supplies, including beads, buttons, decorative flowers, felt, and ribbons.

Darice
www.darice.com
Extensive range of art and craft supplies, including felt, pompoms, sequins, buttons, ribbons, glitters, glues, and paints.

Hobby Lobby
www.hobbylobby.com
Excellent selection of sewing supplies, notions, ribbons, trims, and buttons.

Ikea
www.ikea.com/us
Superstore with a good range of home-decoration, fabric, and baking supplies.

Jo-Ann Fabrics & Crafts
www.joann.com
Wide selection of fabric, sewing, and craft supplies, as well as jewelry-making materials and beads.

Michaels
www.michaels.com
Good range of sewing, needlework, and craft materials.

M&J Trimming
www.mjtrim.com
Lovely selection of decorative trims, notions, ribbons, lace, and buttons.

The Home Depot
www.homedepot.com
Good selection of home-decorating supplies, including paints and fabrics, and tools such as glue guns.

UNITED KINGDOM

CALICO CRAFTS
www.calicocrafts.co.uk
Online crafts specialist with large stock of crafting materials.

CREATIONS ART AND CRAFT MATERIALS
01326 555777
www.ecreations.co.uk
Online craft store with large stock of stencils, paints, brushes, modelling clay and glues as well as plain and decorative papers and a selection of card.

IKEA
Visit www.ikea.com for a catalog or details of your nearest store.

HOBBYCRAFT
0800 027 2384
Visit www.hobbycraft.co.uk for details of your nearest store. Chain of craft superstores carrying everything the crafter needs.

HOMECRAFTS DIRECT
www.homecrafts.co.uk
0116 269 7733
The UK's largest arts and crafts suppliers.

LONDON GRAPHIC CENTRE
020 7759 4500
www.londongraphics.co.uk
The leading suppliers of material to the art and graphic community.

index

Page numbers in bold denote project templates.

Acknowledgments

A big thank you to Penny Wincer for her stunning photographs for the book and for her inspirational ideas for projects too.

Thank you to Hobbycraft for supplying many of the wonderful materials used in the projects throughout the book.

Finally, thank you to my husband Michael and my daughters Jessica and Anna, for putting up with all the mess I created when working on the projects at home!